GOOD MORNING FATHER, GOOD MORNING SON, GOOD MORNING HOLY SPIRIT

CARZADEAN BAKER HARRIS

GOOD MORNING FATHER, GOOD MORNING SON, GOOD MORNING HOLY SPIRIT

Biblical verses are taken from various translations of The Holy Bible.

Published by WHEN HEAVEN SPEAKS, LLC
Post Office Box 55
Pooler, GA 31322
www.whenheavenspeakspublishing.com

GOOD MORNING FATHER, GOOD MORNING SON, GOOD MORNING HOLY SPIRIT

1st Print Edition *Carzadean Baker Harris*

ISBN: 979-8-218-01372-1

Printed in the United States of America

FIRST PAPERBACK EDITION

DEDICATED TO THE MEMORY OF MY MOMMY

"Good Morning Father, Good Morning Son, Good Morning Holy Spirit" is dedicated to the life of my dearly departed mother, Mrs. Lucille Elizabeth "Peggy" Houston Tanksley (06/26/31-02/23/2021)

Mommy, your leadership, nurturing, and love endure forever. I began praying (10/4/2019) and asking the Father to please allow me to finish this project while you yet lived. Well February 23, 2021, you departed from this life, though God did not allow you to be sustained until such a time as this, I honor Him for your memories and the life that you continue to live through me and each member of your legacy.

It is truly a blessing from the Lord, our God Almighty, as still I hear you even now saying as we would depart from one another or end our daily phone conversations, "Talk to you later, Josie," followed by, "If life lasts, and I pray it does." The last time I held your hand and bid you farewell, I spoke those words for you and me, "If life lasts and I pray it does." It didn't last…but it will go on.

Your ongoing push for me to do this as we would talk of the vision behind it, your total belief in whom God had become in my life, and the ministry He entrusted to me and "Your boy Bill", is still encouraging. You attentively listened as I'd read some of the writings, and simply respond with, "This is good. This is God. You can do this Josie." Then, I'd hear you say each time, "I'm so proud of you." This wasn't always expressed with your words, but sometimes simply with just the look of pride on your face, and a hug or grabbing of my hand. His will, your hope, is done.

ALSO DEDICATED TO THE MEMORIES OF...

Mrs. Kimberly Ann Chappell-Stevens, my sister-friend and mentor, my initial editor and reader who set me on track to, "write every day, and set aside a time for us to correspond each week."

Mr. Freddie C. Houston, my uncle-daddy, who encouraged me to look beyond others' eyes and see myself for who I wanted to be.

Mrs. Shirley Ann Harrell, my mother-in-love, who exemplified writing at its best through the scriptures and beyond.

Mr. Charles David Houston & Mr. Joseph Alexander Baker, III., my big brothers as God saw fit for them to be instrumental in my life.

- Carzadean

TABLE OF CONTENTS

About The Cover

The cover is inspired by my morning greeting of gratitude for each day of life, and my mother's appreciation and green thumb for plants of every kind. Thanksgiving Day of 2020, 3 months before my mother passed, she spoke a blessing over this orchid, which had not bloomed for 4 years. Low and behold, 3 months later, 3 days after her passing, a new bloom appeared! Mother's Day 2021, 3 months later the orchid was in full bloom with 5 beautiful flowers. The orchid on the cover is actually "Mommy's Orchid".

ACKNOWLEDGMENTS

God revealed my gift of writing at an early age in my life. It took many years to birth this "vision" of actually sharing my gift in a book for others to experience the calming effect of releasing thoughts to paper and pen. As such, I would like to first thank my God for the inspirations that He gives me daily. The way He leads me through His paths of righteousness, and I write, for His name's sake. It is because of the inspiration of the Father, through the Son, and the encouragement of the Holy Spirit that this book has been made possible for you the reader to experience.

To my husband, William, you most of all, have patiently waited for me to do what needed to be done. Thank you for being my encouragement, my editor in chief, and my faithful reader. Thank you for always considering me and the time I needed to spend in the Lord's presence for Him to be able to fulfill my dream and His vision for me.

To my daughter, Jolene J., for pushing me to be a finisher. For the role you have taken on as my personal life coach. Your God given gift of coaching extends to your family and beyond. Thank you for sharing your skill and expertise in my completion of this effort. For believing long before I started this venture that I could and should do it, my 1st reader in life.

To Jackie, my best friend of more than 48 years. Thank you, my 'Jack', my true BFF, for always being there. You not only entrusted both of your children to my care as their Godmother, but you have expressed a love and belief in the God in me, looking beyond my many faults and helping to fulfill my needs. For every push and encouragement in good times and not so good times, I thank you for staying by my side.

To my pastors, my spiritual leaders, my family, my good friends, Pastors Paul and Lesley Taylor. How can I say thanks, for the things that God has done through your longtime and faithful encouragement in my spiritual walk and growth in Him. Your continual prayers and uplifting are duly noted as I embarked upon and worked to complete this leg of my journey. Thanks to 'Team Taylor' for the push needed to get this book to a published state.

To each of my children, inclusive of my blended family and God children: (Jolene, Trey, Tyhescia, Alexus, Will, Kyle, Tonika), every single one of my siblings (Brenda, Lawanda, Gloria, Lauretta, Karen, Juanita, Charlesetta, Cornelia "Connie", Carolyn "Baby Girl", Gerald), all my exceptional nieces and nephews, family members, friends, supporters and followers, thank you for the encouragement, and inspiration. Even when you didn't realize you were doing it, you continued to inspire me through your life challenges, your triumphs, and victories.

To Author Twylia G. Reid and Heaven Speaks Publishing, you stepped in right on time. I know that the intervention of the Holy Spirit put us together in His time, and not ours. Author Twylia, you have encouraged and guided the fruition of this vision to come forth at its best. Thank you for believing in the book from our very first encounter as author and publisher. The commitment of prayers each time we met, ensured the ordaining of this for the present and the future, and of many more to come.

FOREWORD

From our first class together at Armstrong State College to now, Pastor Carzadean Harris and I have been blessed with a strong bond of sisterhood! We have spent so much time studying, laughing, learning, praying, graduating, and teaching together. I am beyond honored to write this foreword and share with you my thoughts on Pastor Harris' debut book, "Good Morning Father, Good Morning Son, Good Morning Holy Spirit"!

As a writer, she presents real-world examples and shares transparency-through-words which seem to leap off of the pages! As a spirit-led educator, Pastor Harris teaches us the art of studying the scriptures in a simplistic way. She then uses the heart of the text to take us from observation to interpretation that ultimately leads us to application of the Word of God in our everyday lives.

Pastor Harris further provides a relevant view into the word of God that personally expanded my knowledge of the scriptures and provoked me to make immediate applications in my life. A few of the entries that significantly touched me include: *Thankful Means Thank You, Think About it, Make a Choice (Parts 1 & 2), & The Final Piece.* One of my favorite quotes is when she says, *"My time, my season, my puzzle pieces are still evolving"*. It reminds me that our lives are still on a God-ordained journey and aligns with Jeremiah 29:11 (*"For I know the thoughts that I think toward you, says the Lord, thoughts of peace and not of evil, to give you a future and a hope."*).

With all of you in mind, she sought God's direction for a way to be a dynamic blessing to the world. Through this prolific book, I believe that she has truly made God proud and has made the beauty of her ancestors shine brightly. I can only imagine the smile on Sis. Lucille Tanksley's face right now, looking down from heaven as her daughter signs her first written work!

I encourage every reader to use this study text to become a stronger student of the Word and allow the Holy Spirit to speak to you as it has spoken to me!

Lesley S. Taylor
Director of School Improvement
Savannah Chatham Public Schools

INTRODUCTION

This book is inspired by the many inspirational writings endowed through the Holy Spirit as encouragements to the author's Facebook followers, friends, family, and the public at large. I began writing inspirations and encouragements on my personal FB page many years ago. My first evidence of "this notion" was an entry written December 25, 2013 with a salutation of "Good Morning Father, Happy Birthday Son, Have a blessed day Holy Spirit." As time evolved, I began to use my personal morning greeting, "Good Morning Father. Good Morning Son. Good Morning Holy Spirit." to begin my daily posts.

The title of the book reflects on my morning routine of waking and heading downstairs to start each morning. I give honor to the Father for another day of life and seek to face each day with a positive attitude. Seeing the need for others' encouragement, as well as my own, I sought guidance in prayer to respond through my gift of writing and exhortation. The many posts of happiness, sadness, thoughtfulness, and also sometimes, discouragement, motivated me to continue my daily posts. Even in ministry, the worship services begin with my daily greeting of the Trinity in exhortation and praises.

The various topics throughout are inspired by the needs and desires of others. Yet they come from a personal "REAL-ationship" that I have developed with God for many years of my life. The daily life situations and circumstances of people longing for God's attention, mercy, and grace, caught my attention in ways that only He is able to heal and deliver us from.

Although there are many inspirational books available, this book is unique in its layout. It reflects the idea of the Precept© design of Inductive Bible Study. The Word of God therein inspires the reflections. Each entry includes three elements.

1. **Observation** - The scriptures tell the story. Each scripture identified comes from the Holy Bible using various versions. *"What does it say?"*
2. **Interpretation** - Testimonials of life/personal and intimate experiences through the eyes of the author and others. *"What does it mean?"*
3. **Application** – "Journaling My Thoughts" - A journal section where the reader is able to apply their personal thoughts based on the Observation & Interpretation of the entry. *"How can I apply it to my daily living?"*

As the reader, you will not only be enlightened, encouraged, and blessed by the entries, but you will be able to become an active part of the testimonial as you relate each entry to your own personal triumphs. Each three-part entry encourages the reader to get in touch with God through prayer and meditation, but also to grab life by the horns and ride through each situation with confidence, coming out with praise. The reader is encouraged to take one entry at a time, and to meditate on each as necessary.

As you pick up this copy of "*Good Morning Father, Good Morning Son, Good Morning Holy Spirit*", start each day with a prayer to the Father for strength, through the Son, who will be with you, and to be led by the Holy Spirit as your guide.

Included at the culmination of this book are some writings from years gone by, which were written to encourage others through the inspiration of God, and the gift of poetic writing. They tell a story, each totally independent of the other.

This book is meant to encourage and inspire the reader to start each day with a positive attitude, while seeking guidance from the Holy Trinity. It is also meant to provide insight on how to apply scripture to real-life situations.

Designed to be used as a tool to enhance your personal relationship with God, the entries are arranged in such a way that they can be used for individual or group study.

As you move through each of the entries, you are encouraged to reflect on your own experiences and to journal your thoughts, feelings, and insights.

Whether you are new to the Christian faith or have been walking with God for many years, this book will help you deepen your relationship with the Father, Son, and Holy Spirit.

This book is for anyone who is looking for encouragement from the Word of God. It is also for those who are seeking to grow in their relationship with God, and to develop a stronger prayer life. This book would be especially beneficial for those who are going through difficult times, or who are struggling with personal issues. Readers are encouraged to approach each daily entry as a personal challenge, and to use the "Application" element and the journaling section at the end of the book to reflect on their own thoughts and experiences.

OBSERVATION

"Trust in the Lord, and do good; so shalt thou dwell in the land, and verily thou shalt be fed. Delight thyself also in the Lord: and he shall give thee the desires of thine heart. Commit thy way unto the Lord; trust also in him; and he shall bring it to pass." **Psalms 37: 3-5 (KJV)**

"IT'S PRAYER TIME"

Prayer – a direct line of communication for the purpose of making petitions and worshiping God.

INTERPRETATION

Good Morning Father. Good Morning Son. Good Morning Holy Spirit. Father if we may be allowed to approach your throne even at this appointed time, Lord, we'd be ever so grateful. This morning we're pleading the Blood of Jesus over every situation and every circumstance. We're pleading the Blood of our Savior in our land and country. Throughout this world God, we're pleading the healing power of Jesus through every stripe that He took for us. In this community, in our homes, and over our families, we're pleading the Blood of the Lamb to free the captive and set them free.

We're pleading in prayer, and we're praying in season and out of season. It was you Lord who said, *"If my people called by my name would humble themselves, pray, seek my face, and turn from their wicked ways, then you would hear from heaven, forgive their sins, and heal their land."* We're standing on your word, on your promises.

Dear Father, you reminded us in Psalm 37:4 and Matthew 6:33 to delight ourselves in you, to seek you and your righteousness. If we'd do these things, the desires of our hearts would be fulfilled. All things would be added to us. This is every need and every desire in your will and for our sake. We only pray that we've delighted in you enough. That we've become content with what you've given us and where you have us and how you've blessed us in and of our lives. We pray that we've sought your ways enough to make you happy, Lord.

We know and believe that all things do work for the good of us who love you and are called according to your purpose. Let us place your purpose at the forefront of our hearts and minds. We're pleading the Blood of Jesus for strength, encouragement, and direction. Thank you Father. Thank you, Son. Thank you, Holy Spirit. In the name of Jesus Christ, our Lord and Savior, we pray and we say amen and amen.

APPLICATION

Whatever your needs or desires are, making your prayer life a priority gives open access to building that "REAL-ationship" with the Father. Write about how you feel about prayer and what you know it can do in your life.

OBSERVATION

"O LORD our Lord, how excellent is thy name in all the earth! Who hast set thy glory above the heavens."

Psalm 8:1 (KJV)

"GOD IS EXCELLENCE"

Everything that God created and brings forth is in excellence. Even more so, this scripture exclaims that the Lord's name is excellent in all the earth. It doesn't matter our name in the world, nor our position or status. It doesn't matter where we physically reside, be it near or far, or where our emotional being is living. What does matter is that God is a Spirit, and we must worship Him in "*spirit and truth*".

INTERPRETATION

God's name is excellent in all the earth. That is among the heathen as well as the saved. The spirit of the Lord living in us begets excellence. To exhibit excellence means, "to possess outstanding quality or superior merit." So, when we "Live in Excellence" God resides in us. That's right! He chooses to be a part of us. This means that you are '*somehow*' remarkably good. And, that '*somehow*' is the spirit of the Lord.

As people of God, or people in general, we strive to do good or live right each day. What is right if it is not righteousness? Righteousness breeds holiness, and holiness is of God. If we profess to be of God then as His people we must represent Him by living in and through His Word. Even those of us who may not profess Him, there is something always nagging us to do right or to do better. The Word of God is our guide to holy and righteous living.

This representation that I speak of, must be in all we say, and in all we do. This, my friend, is excellence. Everything that comes forth from us should have His purpose in mind. His purpose for us is to praise Him. He expects this from us each day in the form of excellence. Our motto at RHEMA Christian Fellowship Ministry Virtual Community Church is: *Living in Excellence, We Walk in Expectation.* We believe fully that God gives us the desires of our hearts when we follow His lead to righteousness.

APPLICATION

Are there any situations that you have experienced in your life that exemplify God's excellence? Write about those experiences, as you remember and relish them.

OBSERVATION

"No weapon that is formed against you will prosper; and every tongue that accuses you in judgment, you will condemn. This is the heritage of the servants of the Lord, and their vindication is from Me," declares the Lord."

Isaiah 54:17 (NASB 1995)

"AMONG THOSE CALLED, FEW ARE CHOSEN"

Those chosen by the Most High God have inherited their clearance of all accusations and suspicions brought forth by the enemy. We have dealt with many things unexpected, unexplained, unwarranted, undesirable, and unnecessary. As the chosen of the Lord we can choose to say to these things with confidence, "*Fine. So what! God's got this, and me." "I condemn and don't believe a word you say.*"

INTERPRETATION

Your chosen status gives you certain rights and privileges that eliminate threats before they materialize. Even in the minds of those who may be used to plot against you, they will see God working it out on your behalf. Your heritage was bequeathed as a blessing for living in and through Him. For His glorification and your salvation, God vindicated and forgave you when Christ went to the cross. Exercise your right to live above and beyond the reckless and negative expectations or thoughts of others, the condemnation of man, and live for the victory in Christ Jesus.

Through circumstances that seem beyond your control, God has already prepared you for the battle. When it seems all is lost and there is no rebuilding, no restructuring, or no hope, God has preordered your next stride and ordained every step to be a building block towards your success. So, characteristic of your calling, you've been chosen to stand boldly, and having done all, to stand.

APPLICATION

Reflect on a time when you went through a hardship and though it seemed nothing was going your way, somehow things worked out in your favor. Recap and reminisce on that time as you refresh your thoughts of how God chose to bless you, in spite of the hardship.

OBSERVATION

"The LORD answered, "My presence will go with you and I will give you peace." **Exodus 33:14 (GWT)**

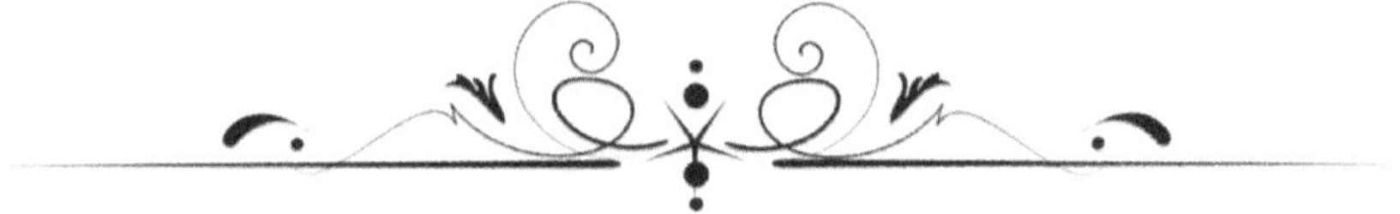

"KEEPER OF HIS PEACE"

God will forever be present. Even if Heaven and Earth pass away, God will still be here. The world was wiped clean as the rains flooded the earth and God performed a physical cleansing of man and his iniquities. Imagine Noah as the rain begins to fall and fall, and keeps falling. Worried! Concerned! Yet peace abideth.

INTERPRETATION

Imagine us, as God cleans up our messes time after time. He washes us up just as He washed the earth in Noah's time. As then, and now, we sometimes revert back to a dirty and unwashed state of mind or living. You would think we could control ourselves better. You would think this time we'd get it right. Might we know that His peace stays when we allow His presence?

But time after time, we face situations and find or feel that we don't have His peace. God provides us with His peace daily, yet we seemingly are unable to keep it for long. Why is this? Because we give it up. Why? Because we won't let God truly lead every decision we make, and every step we take. Why? We don't trust Him enough to receive His peace and keep it. If our faith is not fed through our belief and trust that God's will is to remain with us, it dwindles, and so does our peace.

He so freely provides for all of us His peace, which surpasses all understanding. The truth of the matter is that "God Can", and we "Can Do All Things Through Him Who Strengthens Us". We continue to deal with all of this, simply because we forget that God is forever with us, omnipresent in every situation, and keeping us in His perfect place of peace.

APPLICATION

God is a very present help in our time of need and provides us with peace from day to day. Focus on walking in peace each day. What steps can you take to do your part in keeping that peace?

OBSERVATION

"God is not unjust; he will not forget your work and the love you have shown Him as you have helped his people and continue to help them." **Hebrews 6:10 (NIV)**

"MY GREATER REWARD IS IN HIM"

Whatever you do for good, God will reward. It may seem to go unnoticed in this world. Things you do may seem to be overlooked at your job and in your home. The rewards and awards may be few and far between. It may seem that others are always being recognized and lifted up for the world to see. You might not ever be recognized for any accomplishment in your lifetime here on earth.

INTERPRETATION

Please know that God is noticing every effort on your part and your reward from Him will be greater than any reward or award that man can recognize you with. Don't get caught up with what others may or may not feel compelled to give recognition to. Continue to see about, encourage, and even give to others in need. This is the Will of God in Christ Jesus concerning you. Take His command to "*Love thy neighbor as thyself*" with a realness and seriousness that others may or may not understand. Don't look for "Thank You". It may never come.

You may never be chosen as the "Person of the Year". But remember that you are God's chosen for life. The prestige of the world, the church people, and the job association may never speak of your deeds as if they have made a difference. But His word says to "*Be not weary in your well-doing, for in due season you shall reap what you have sown.*" Just keep doing what you do. Help here and assist there. God's greater is bigger than the world at large. I declare and decree that this day, while you walk in His perfect peace that "*greater is He in you than He that is in the world.*" Simply put, your 'greater' is on the way. Your 'greater' is coming!

APPLICATION

Reflect on a time/event where you worked hard; even above and beyond what was expected, yet no one even said "*Thank you*". Maybe you felt used? Or perhaps you felt that the recipient of your hard work was ungrateful? Write about how you really felt and why.

OBSERVATION

"When this corruptible is clothed with incorruptibility, and this mortal is clothed with immortality, then the saying that is written will take place: Death has been swallowed up in victory. Death, where is your sting? Death, where is your victory? Now the sting of death is sin, and the power of sin is the law. But thanks be to God, who gives us the victory through our Lord Jesus Christ!"

1 Corinthians 15: 54-57 (HCSB)

"DEATH IS ON THE MOVE – BUT LIFE IS ABOUNDING"

Times are very trying right now. It seems that "Death" is on a prowl. Day in and day out the spirit of death is falling everywhere. It creeps into our beds at night. It calls our name walking down the street. It slides into the car next to us when we're driving. It's even so bold as to go to church with us. It follows our children from home to school and back. Death visits everywhere and it is letting its presence be known worldwide.

INTERPRETATION

Death comes when death is ready. Sometimes death shows us that it's coming. Yet we can't stop the inevitable of death's arrival. We cry that the streets are taking our children, yet we choose to assist death with their apprehension. Brothers killing brothers. Sisters setting each other up for the kill. Mothers and even Fathers take no thought in snuffing out the life of an innocent and helpless child, even their own. We mourn the loss with extreme hurt and pain. Yet, we give death a helping hand. Lord have mercy on us all!

Death will come, and is coming. It seeks to be fulfilled. It will not have mercy. It will come again and again and again. Death seeks the lost as well as the found. But God! Our Kind and Loving, Merciful and Great God. He will have Mercy. He has given us victory over death. Though we die in Christ, Saints of God, yet shall we live? Death is temporary for those of us in the Lord.

Bring your family in from death's way. Dying is for those who are lost in sin. Life is for those who are saved in Jesus, the Christ, the Way, the Truth, and the Life. Take a moment each day to close death's door and open the pathway to life, and to live it more abundantly.

Him, the Way, the Truth, the Life. Because of our belief in Him our salvation defies death's plan. Because He lives, death can only bring a deep sleep upon us. "The Dead in Christ Shall Rise First". Victory in Jesus means that death has no sting. Death has no victory. The word of God reminds us that, "*He that is free in Christ, is free indeed.*" Free from sin. Free from death. Choose Christ. Choose life.

APPLICATION

You've lost a loved one and the hurt is still very real. Take some time to write them a note of what your heart is going through. This exercise can help you gain some relief or closure for your loss.

OBSERVATION

"For my thoughts are not your thoughts, neither are your ways my ways, saith the Lord. For as the heavens are higher than the earth, so are my ways higher than your ways, and my thoughts than your thoughts."

Isaiah 55: 8-9 (KJV)

"UNFATHOMABLE, BUT REAL"

Sometimes, even when we know what God is capable of it's still hard for us to fathom His power. When we've experienced God's power work in our lives you'd think that we'd have our faith game together. You'd think that after all He's done we would believe Him without hesitation. Hmmmm... But do we really?

INTERPRETATION

It's not necessarily that we don't believe God for what He can and will do. But the reach of His power can seem to supersede or be above and beyond our highest level of "I Believe". Situations and circumstances that overrule our common sense, or what we make of things, can leave us confused and at the edge of not being sure of the outcome of it all. So when God does what he does, and comes through, we're once again left in awe of Him.

The faith we have in His ability to do anything and everything is beyond our highest level of human confidence in Him. So don't be weary if you happen to wonder or even question situations that seem impossible. Just remember that with God all things are possible. Be reminded that He doesn't do it the way we do it. Nor does He think about it the way we think about it.

Recording artist, Esther F. Perkins, wrote & sang with E. Larry McDuffie & the Savannah Community Choir, "*God is real, I know I feel Him deep down in my soul. No matter what the price may be, He's able to fix it for me. When down to my last dime, He steps right in on time. He's all that I need, God is real. Yes, my God is real.*"

He's God, He always has been, and will continue to be unfathomable, but very, very, real!

APPLICATION

Does God keep solving issues in your life, yet you worry about what comes next? Take a moment and reflect on the mercy and grace he has extended to you over time.

OBSERVATION

"Rejoice in hope, be patient in tribulation, be constant in prayer." **Romans 12:12 (NIV)**

"I'M SO GLAD TROUBLE DON'T LAST ALWAYS"

One of my favorite personal sayings goes like this, "*No Matter what it Looks Like, Sounds Like, or Feels Like, God is Still in Control*". I realize that if I'm to make it in this life, I have no choice but to trust God. I must totally rely on His choices for my life. I understand that even when I'm going through tribulations, God is perfectly aware. He hasn't left me nor forsaken me. And He will do for me what He has done time after time; He will bring me through every given situation, into a renewed place of peace.

INTERPRETATION

Many times in our lives, we seem to completely forget or feel uncertain of whether God is really with or for us. That's because we allow what we see, hear, and feel to affect us internally with external issues. Get out of your own head and get into the word and presence of God. Stop over thinking God's intentions. His will for our lives is intentional in every way.

Whatever God allows us to face or deal with, please try to remember that He is already on the other side of it. He gives hope through our own testimonies and the hope and testimonies of others. Our breakthrough is just a matter of time away. He's there with us while dealing with every situation and circumstance. Just be patient and wait. "*Wait I say on the Lord and be of good courage*!"

While you're waiting, stay before Him. Pray without ceasing. Keep the faith. God is simply doing what God does and can and will do. God is seeing you through. He's holding the enemy at bay and daring him to cross the line. You may be tried but God is true. So, rejoice in knowing that the victory is already yours. Be patient in the hard times, knowing they won't last always. Stay prayerful my brothers and sisters, Our Father Who art in Heaven, is listening. He does hear and answer prayer.

APPLICATION

On time God? Yes, He Is! Reflect on a time(s) that God came through for you; the situation worked out. Even if it wasn't the way you were expecting, it happened right on time.

OBSERVATION

"For the Lord God is a sun and shield; The Lord gives grace and glory; He withholds no good thing from those who walk with integrity." **Psalm 84:11 (NASB)**

"YOUR GREATER IS COMING"

When we try hard to do good and remain humble, God's grace and glory covers us and produces blessings greater than any we've ever imagined. Whenever we choose good or we do good, God rewards us with greater. God's Word reminds us that He rains on the just as well as the unjust. Meaning that even when we do falter and perhaps don't make the best choices, we still receive blessings galore. However, when we are intentional about living in integrity and representing the Kingdom, we are rewarded with the greater of these very blessings.

INTERPRETATION

Sometimes we find ourselves feeling less than deserving of the many blessings coming our way. Other times we find ourselves wondering when we'll get a breakthrough. Because we've cleaned up our act and turned our lives around, God chooses to bless us with our greater. Don't try to justify why the blessings are flowing or not flowing, just receive them when they do flow and trust that God is shielding and protecting you; not holding back any good thing or holding old things against you.

My cousin, gospel recording artist, the late Barbara Ann Green McCoy would sing with conviction the song, "Only What You Do for Christ Will Last". Each time I heard her, it would build my confidence in knowing that my choices to glorify Him in my living, were not being done in vain. I can still hear Barbara's angelic voice singing as she blessed us with another song, "Somebody Bigger Than You and I". God is bigger and greater than anything we face or lack or can receive on this earth. Because He is greater, I can receive what's greater. Hang in there and keep doing good. Your greater is on the way.

APPLICATION

Do you sometimes find yourself not wanting to do something to help someone because of a past mistake they made? Consider what might help you to get past that feeling and stop holding it against them.

OBSERVATION

"Have confidence in your leaders and submit to their authority, because they keep watch over you as those who must give an account. Do this so that their work will be a joy, not a burden, for that would be of no benefit to you. Pray for us. We are sure that we have a clear conscience and desire to live honorably in every way."

Hebrews 13:17-18 (NIV)

"EVEN ME LORD, LET SOME DROPS FALL ON ME"

As a pastor and preacher, and lover and teacher of the Word of God, sometimes I need to be refreshed. Kingdom leaders need the people of God to lift them up. We need prayers going forth on our behalf. We need to be encouraged and not discouraged. We need to be lifted up and not torn down. We need armor bearers who will stand with us when we've done all to stand and yet we still stand. We need a word from the Lord.

INTERPRETATION

Let Us Pray. Lord, please send down the rain on your servants who serve and lead your Kingdom, through your wisdom, knowledge, and understanding. Refresh their anointing with fresh drops from Heaven. Continue to be the lifter up of their heads.

Send into the congregations of the faithful, those who desire you, and only you. Send those who will cover your men and women of God in prayer through fasting and supplication. Oh Lord, bring into the fold lost souls that they too might be saved. Allow angels unknown to our natural eyes to keep watch for snakes lying in wait to strike against them. Let no weapons form that are intended to do them harm. Anointing of the one and only true, and living God, fall afresh on your people this day at this very hour. In the mighty, matchless, name of our Lord and Savior, Jesus Christ, we pray. Amen and amen.

APPLICATION

How often do you take time to pray for, or intervene in the spirit for your pastors or spiritual leaders (even for your earthly leaders)? Reflect on how you can support them through prayers and support in a manner that will be uplifting to the work and the sacrifices they make each day in ministry.

OBSERVATION

"I will give thanks to you, Lord, with all my heart; I will tell of all your wonderful deeds. I will be glad and rejoice in you; I will sing the praises of your name, O Most High."

Psalm 9:1-2 (NIV)

"THANKFUL TO SAY, THANK YOU"

Too often we go from day to day without ever saying these two simple words. "Thank you." These two effortless words can mean so much. But, most importantly they mean that you're blessed, and you appreciate the blessing. "*Thank you*" is simply a humble response to what you just received.

INTERPRETATION

At a time in my life when I was experiencing serious hardship my job barely paid enough to pay the section 8 rent, and whatever else was needed. I was paying for gas in my car with rolled coins hidden in the closet from myself as a savings account. The bank account was overdrawn, and I literally did not know where the next meal for me and my child was coming from. I questioned my inability to take care of this life entrusted to me. During this time all I could think about was the saying, "*Thank you makes room for more.*" Lord, please send me some more!

One particular day my doorbell rang. To my surprise, it was one of my sisters. She'd unexpectedly showed up with bags of groceries for my daughter and me. With tears in my eyes and a full voice, I said, "*Thank you.*" Over and over again I told her, and the Lord thank you.

I had no idea then and still don't know now, just how she knew what I was going through. Even when you don't think people know what's going on, God is working on your behalf through someone who feels your needs. Don't dwell on what people fail to do or what you don't have. God is coming through, and when He does just say, "*Thank you.*"

She never mentioned it after that day. Because of the thankfulness I had in my heart then and now, it still causes me to tear up as I say, "*To my loving, giving, caring sister, I am forever grateful, and I thank you.*" Listen. I always say, "*Thank God for the now*!"

APPLICATION

Think about the times you used these two words after having received a blessing from someone. Were you appreciative or grateful of what you received? How did it make you feel?

OBSERVATION

"Let us then approach God's throne of grace with confidence, so that we may receive mercy and find grace to help us in our time of need." **Hebrews 4:16 (NIV)**

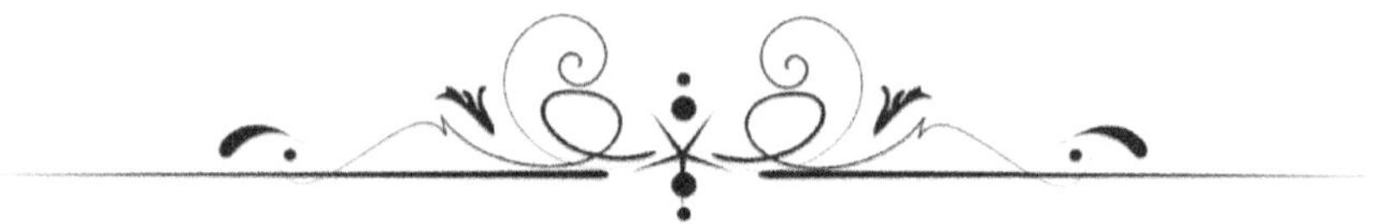

"THE LORD IS BLESSING ME, RIGHT NOW!"

Merriam-Webster defines the word "blessing" as God's favor and protection. All in favor lift your eyes to the hills from where your help comes from. The blessings of the Lord are upon us. We need to make sure we work to stay in His good will. He forever gives us His blessings, mercy, and grace.

INTERPRETATION

As defined by Merriam-Webster, "mercy" is compassion or forgiveness shown toward someone whom it is within one's power to punish or harm. Be grateful that God is not like us. As a people, we sometimes tend to be very punitive when it comes to each other. Mercy is what we, people of God, need to be able to share more of.

Furthermore, Merriam-Webster defines "grace" as the free and unmerited favor of God, as manifested in the salvation of sinners and the bestowal of blessings. Take note, grace was the only one of these three words that was referenced as dealing with Christians.

What if God was to turn the tables of time on you and take back all of the BLESSINGS, MERCY, and GRACE that you have received?

We can always go to the dictionary to “look it up” when unsure of the meaning of a word. But if we "look up" to the hills from where our help comes from, we as Christians, saints of God, people of God, etc. will find that BLESSINGS, MERCY, and GRACE all mean His LOVE and COMPASSION given into our lives abundantly, and *more abundantly*. God has indeed been very tolerable and forgiving even when we know we did not deserve it.

APPLICATION

Think about that person or people whom you refuse or refused to show mercy because of past or present hurt. Describe how you would feel if the tables were turned and *you* were not shown mercy, or didn't receive grace.

OBSERVATION

"Now when the unclean spirit goes out of a man, it passes through waterless places seeking rest, and does not find it. Then it says, 'I will return to my house from which I came'; and when it comes, it finds it unoccupied, swept, and put in order. Then it goes and takes along with it seven other spirits more wicked than itself, and they go in and live there; and the last state of that man becomes worse than the first." **Matthew 12:43-45 (NASB)**

"CHANGE IS YOURS FOR THE ASKING"

When you ask God to "change" you and He cleans you up, please take care of your temple by grooming it with the Word of God daily. You should commune with Him through the blood of Jesus for a daily inner washing. Polish your shining light each morning with praises unto the Father. When He changes you stay in the know of how to remain changed. This comes through continual and daily prayer and communication with Him. This is that REAL-ationship I've been speaking of.

The Apostle Paul reminds us to "*study to show ourselves approved...*" Many of our struggles come because of our ignorance of the Word of God. Delight yourself in Him, and seek first His kingdom and righteousness. Stay clean and don't wallow in the dirt of the past so that Matthew 12:43-45 will *NOT* be your testimony.

INTERPRETATION

There was a time in my life when I was trying to connect with God but just couldn't get it right. God had been dealing with me spiritually about going in and out of His presence when I wanted to do what my flesh was leading me into. The last time I straddled the fence of salvation and the world God literally took His spirit from me. One particular night after my reckless acts of sin, I became very ill. I ended up in the bathroom releasing everything in me from both ends. As this was happening, I was almost at a place of convulsing. At the last heave, I tried to cry out to God. But, He either didn't hear me or chose not to listen.

At that exact moment I felt the presence of God leave my very being. The feeling of desertion of the Holy Spirit left me at rock bottom. I struggled for months trying to get in His presence until He let me know that He'd been there all the time. I had deserted Him, and He couldn't stay within me, because my temple was defiled and filled with many unclean spirits. As such, we've heard so many times, God really does not live in unclean places.

APPLICATION

Are there things going on in your life that you are willing to chance your relationship with God for? If so, how can you work to fix this? If not, what do you need to do to maintain your relationship with Him?

OBSERVATION

"I therefore, the prisoner of the Lord, beseech you that ye walk worthy of the vocation wherewith ye are called, with all lowliness and meekness, with longsuffering, forbearing one another in love; Endeavoring to keep the unity of the Spirit in the bond of peace." **Ephesians 4: 1-3**

"REPRESENT THE GOD WE SERVE"

With a calling on us, our daily endeavors should include acting like, looking like, and being true to the call of being children of Christ. We should find ourselves exemplifying patience, love, and humility even in the toughest of situations.

As we are amongst others and even within ourselves, there is a standard that we must set and live by. That standard has to always be mindful of how we make our Father look to the world at large. Do we look like the God who made us in His image?

INTERPRETATION

Be reminded through this, *"Giving no offence in anything, that the ministry be not blamed: But in all things approving ourselves as the ministers of God, in much patience, in afflictions, in necessities, in distresses, etc."*
2 Corinthians 6: 3-4

Our God is excellent! Thus, we must live in excellence and allow Him to reside in us. This exhibition of excellence means we understand our mission and are able to stay focused on our purpose. Living in that state of being 'somehow remarkably good' keeps presenting itself. The excellence in us comes from the spirit of the Lord and not from anything of our own doing.

Wherever you are, let it be known that you are of God and that He abides in you. Focus on being who God desires you to be. Put away your deceitful ways. Be real with who you are, and who you need to be. Hold on to the God of Excellence and His unchanging hand. Abide in Him and allow His unwavering ways to abide in you. Proclaim excellence in every aspect of your life. Strive each day to live and breathe Excellence. Thus, you will become Excellence. As He is excellent and we are of Him, we too can "Live in Excellence and Walk in Expectation."

APPLICATION

With every new day, you should assess whether your lifestyle is allowing others to see God in you. Reflect on actions that you know represent God, and your actions that haven't represented Him. How can this change?

OBSERVATION

"On that day many will say to me, 'Lord, Lord, did we not prophesy in your name, and cast out demons in your name, and do many mighty works in your name?' And then will I declare to them, I never knew you; depart from me, you workers of lawlessness."

Matthew 7: 22-23 (ESV)

"That he might present it to himself a glorious church, not having spot, or wrinkle, or any such thing; but that it should be holy and without blemish."

Ephesians 5:27 (KJV)

"LIVE LIFE IN THE REAL"

There is no way we can choose to live in our flesh and die with His spirit. God expects that we will follow His lead and live each day to please Him by being faithful enough to believe and trust Him. Our eternal right to life depends on our temporary way of living.

INTERPRETATION

The only way to the Kingdom is through living in and through the will of God in Christ Jesus. Choosing to live in His will and following His commands afford opportunities of blessings from God. This has to be our choice for living in the "Now". Our present state of life will determine our forever state of being. Focus on what you're saying and doing to yourself and others around you each day. Many times, we may unconsciously insult others and even insult God in our words and deeds. But we have to remember each day that God is always looking and listening, and He knows our innermost thoughts and ways.

Stay steadfast. Be unmovable. Be who God has called you to be; true saints, worshiping Him.

"*For them that Worship Him, Must Worship in Spirit and in Truth.*" The Word of God declares that He's coming back for a church (you and I) without spot or wrinkle. Does He really know you? Do you really know Him? Is there a REAL-ationship going on between you, the Father, Son, and Holy Spirit? God is looking for those whom He will proclaim forevermore. He loves you. Do you REAL-ly love Him? If you do, then don't just do the works of the Kingdom but live the life that you preach and teach each day. Live life in the 'REAL' and do it in the 'NOW'.

APPLICATION

Are you sure that you are living in a manner pleasing to the Father; a life that lines up with His will and His way? Take a moment each morning to reflect on, "God's will for me today".

OBSERVATION

"The woman was convinced. She saw that the tree was beautiful and its fruit looked delicious, and she wanted the wisdom it would give her. So she took some of the fruit and ate it..." **Genesis 3:6 (NLT)**

"For God has not given us a spirit of fear, but of power and of love and of a sound mind." **2 Timothy 1:7 (NKJV)**

"THE MIND – THE BATTLEFIELD FOR OUR SPIRIT"

Eve gave in to the temptation to know more. Perhaps even, to have more. A simple "*No, devil,*" would have sufficed. She did not execute her sound mind. She did not use self-control. Just like Eve, we without wisdom, seek answers to all of those *what-if* questions without trusting and consulting God through the Holy Spirit. Sometimes our mind overrules our common sense, which is in my opinion, our Godly sense. If we just go ahead and trust Him and lean not to our own understanding, we'd render the fear within us powerless through the power of God in us. When fear creeps in, it brings hesitation, confusion and a sense of insecurity.

INTERPRETATION

What happens when we're face to face with unexpected circumstances, when we no longer feel self-sufficient or secure in our position? Fear is able to find its place in our heart. God has given us self-control, or our sound mind. We must exercise our right to use it, and to use it wisely. In our heart and mind we must really allow God to lead.

However when we have a mind vs. spirit battle, we begin to over think. I often say, my first mind, is my right mind, is my God mind. Follow your initial thoughts. Eve hesitated, but pressed past her first mind, her right mind, her God mind. I would say for most of us it probably goes something like this:

What if it doesn't work out? What if he/she leaves me? What if something bad happens? What if I lose? Do I have to decide now? What if, what if, what if?

APPLICATION

Focusing on the unknown gives fear an edge. God wants us to release our spirit of fear and trust Him with the plan. What's happening in your life that makes you feel less than adequate, to a point that you experience fear in and of your decisions? List a few ways you can put your trust or faith into action on a daily basis.

OBSERVATION

"And if it seems evil unto you to serve the Lord, choose you this day whom ye will serve; whether the gods which your fathers served that were on the other side of the flood, or the gods of the Amorites, in whose land ye dwell: but as for me and my house, we will serve the Lord."

Joshua 24:15 (KJV)

"THINK ABOUT IT - MAKE A CHOICE" (PART 1)

Listen... As Christians, we can no longer continue to confuse ourselves with the world. Either you're for God or you're not. What is really going on? If the world is in any way confused about our identity as a Christian - NOT A CHURCH GOER - then we need to come up with a "Prayer-Repentance-Restoration-Revival". The world has to come to Him through our representation of God's Kingdom. "Thy Kingdom Come, Thy Will Be Done."

INTERPRETATION

"*Praise God from Whom All Blessings Flow*" comes out of one side of our mouth. In the next instance, we (people of God) are slandering, "throwing shade", or cussing somebody out. You don't even have to use profanity. The very things you say to dig deep or hurt someone is a "cussing out", because you want to make a point, and publicly put them in their place.

The saying, “hurt people, hurt people”, is too often true in the church community. We’ve got to learn to let go and REAL-ly let God. We say this a lot when it comes to boosting the worshippers. But what about making sure that the worship is in “spirit and in truth”. Beware my dear brothers and sisters. Our God is not mocked. If you find yourself putting your religion on the shelf so you can "handle your business", then we have a serious problem!

Hurt feelings don’t justify you using your words to hurt someone in retaliation. Understand that you’re choosing with a clear conscience, whom you will serve. Every one of your actions should represent him in all situations you encounter, in season and out of season.

APPLICATION

According to Joshua 24:15, maybe doing the right thing seems evil to you. So, you choose to do evil, because it seems right at the time. Reflect on a time when you consciously chose to tell someone off or do something to embarrass another person. Even if they were telling you off or had betrayed your feelings, how did you feel afterwards? Did you take it to God for repentance?

OBSERVATION

"And if it seems evil unto you to serve the Lord, choose you this day whom ye will serve; ..." ***Joshua 24:15 (KJV)***

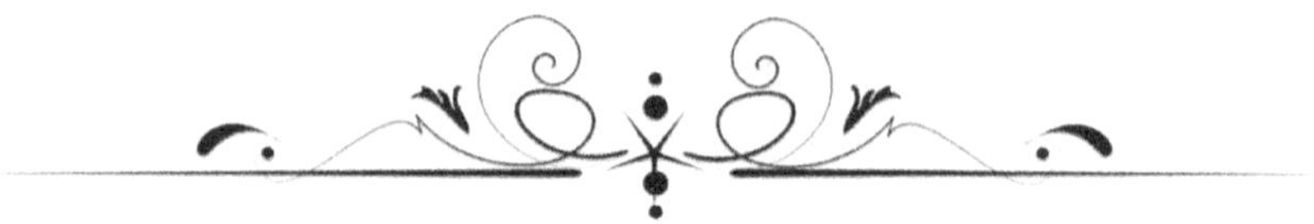

"THINK ABOUT IT - MAKE A CHOICE" (PART 2)

Our decision to not make a choice is indeed, a choice within itself. We may say that we are truly leaning on the Lord's side. Yet, we may often hesitate to do right or say what's true. We don't want to offend or intrude on others' rights and feelings. However, we quickly do wrong and take folks down without a blink because we get caught up with the spirit of foolery that so easily moves about in our atmosphere.

INTERPRETATION

The world will go after every *right* they think is theirs. But, their *"right"* way could lead them straight to hell. There are too many "*rights*" of the people that stand flat-footed and boldfaced against the Word of God. Why can't we Saints of God stand flat-footed and boldfaced for the Word of God?

What about our rights as followers of Christ? Believe me when I tell you the world could care less who knows what side they're on. But we, people of God, are often not sure of what to do in any given situation. Remember the devil comes to steal, kill, and destroy. So, if he can halt our prayers, calling on Jesus, and trusting God, just for a moment, he can gain victory before we know it.

We shy away from letting folks know we are saved by the blood of Jesus Christ, and love the Lord our God with all of our heart, mind, and soul for fear they will call us "religious". The audacity of church folk who mindlessly joke with each other saying things like "*You're too saved for me*." I don't find this to be a laughing matter in any shape, form, or fashion. We fail daily to "*Live in Excellence, and Walk in Expectation*" because we want to fit in. We're always busy trying to run a hustle rather than working diligently to gain souls for the Kingdom. I'll say it again, God cannot be mocked. We're either going to trust Him or sway from side to side until the pendulum of life stops, or Christ returns and we find ourselves on the outs.

We can no longer continue to confuse ourselves with the world. The world knows exactly who they are. Choose this day, whose side you are on.

APPLICATION

Either you are for God or you are not. You will either choose to live for Him or you will choose to die. The choice truly is yours. What's your choice? Write about it and why?

OBSERVATION

"These things I have spoken to you, so that in Me you may have peace. In the world you have tribulation but take courage; I have overcome the world."

John 16:33 (NASB 1995)

"I can do all things through Christ who strengthens me."

Philippians 4:13 (NKJV)

"SPOKEN PEACE STRENGTHENS"

Our peace may come in different ways, but it all comes from the same source. When Christ died, He rose, and when he got up, He got up with all power in His Hands. Because of Him, we should no longer have to worry or fret. But because of our human nature, sometimes we still do.

INTERPRETATION

The more you seek peace, the more you shall find. But beware of the enemy coming to steal it, kill it, and destroy it if he can. The moment you declare peace the devil will try to disrupt, wreak havoc, and cause confusion. Hold on to God's unchanging hand. He's going to come through.

Day in and day out we continue to live through the ups and downs of life. As we approach each situation or circumstance, we're reminded in the scriptures that Christ overcame the world for us. Simply said the worries of and about the things we face have no power in disrupting our peace. It is up to us to recognize these issues and use the courage provided to hold on to our peace. Tribulations and daily struggles are not hidden or camouflaged from us. We see them coming head on.

This is truly a reality for me as I reflect during a time when I was faced with taking exams, pursuing various degrees and certification in education. Each time I sat for these exams I would write out the words to Philippians 4:13 on a sticky note. I would place the note at the top right corner of the desk where I sat. At any time I found myself struggling with an answer or response, I would take a moment and silently read this scripture. I would instantly receive a sense of peace and an ability to regain my focus.

APPLICATION

In life, there will be situations that sometimes seem hard or impossible to overcome or accomplish. Can you come up with a strategy to use the scriptures to help you stay calm and live in a place of peace?

OBSERVATION

"Now therefore, I pray you, if I have found grace in your sight, show me now your way, that I may know you, that I may find grace in your sight: and consider that this nation is your people." **Exodus 33:13 (KJV)**

"CONSIDER ME"

From day to day, we need the Lord to consider who we are. We must thus remember to always consider God's ways.

INTERPRETATION

Consider who I am
Consider my ways oh Lord
My direction, my comprehension, and the way I travel
The way I must go.

Consider who I Am
Consider my ways thy child
The way I bless you, the way I keep you
The way I cover you and the direction I'm sending you in.

Consider who I am
Called by your name, humbling myself in prayer
In need of forgiveness, standing for what's right
Shunned at times for righteousness sake
Yet, a heart for you my Lord.

Consider who I Am
Teach transgressors my ways

Preach my Word throughout the days
Alpha and Omega, Author and Finisher of thy faith
Lily of the Valley, Bright and Morning Star
Each day I hand you brand new mercies, and My Amazing Grace.

"I AM WHO I AM, THE LORD YOUR GOD. AND YES, YOU ARE MY CHILD."

APPLICATION

As you read the words of this poetic piece, what thoughts were going through your mind? This is a personal conversation between the writer and the Father. How do you share your thoughts with Him?

OBSERVATION

"Therefore, the promise comes by faith, so that it may be by grace and may be guaranteed to all Abraham's offspring--not only to those who are of the law but also to those who have the faith of Abraham. He is the father of us all. As it is written: "I have made you a father of many nations." He is our father in the sight of God, in whom he believed--the God who gives life to the dead and calls into being things that were not." ***Romans 4: 16-17 (NIV)***

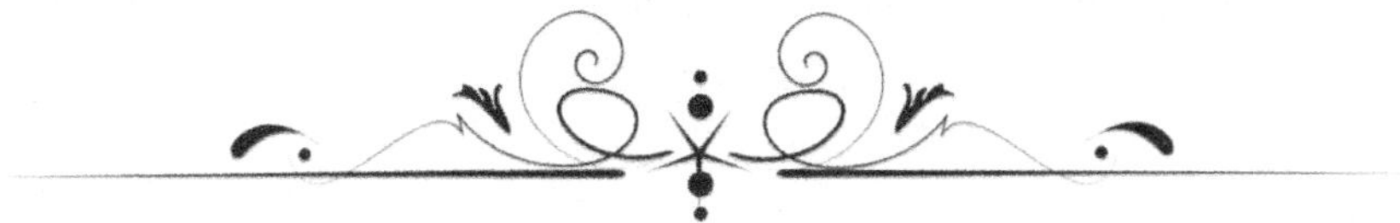

"GOD SPOKE, NOW SPEAK"

Our Father has endowed us with His power to do all things through Christ who strengthens us. God ordained Abraham's life to father a nation of people who would walk in the newness of life. God spoke blessings over generations of people through speaking over and through the life of one man. He is that kind of God.

INTERPRETATION

In your home. On your job. Around your community.
Across this land and country. Throughout this world.
Speak to the atmosphere.

Humbled but not humiliated. Blessed yet not stressed.
I am created by Him who keeps me, but certainly not berated by any means. As you speak in season, and out of season speak to the atmosphere. This day, speak those things that might not be as if they already are. The

declaration that God did this is found in Romans 4:17 as Abraham received the blessing of nations. Abraham became the recipient for a nation.

Love and not hate. Adore and not abhor. Present do not resent. Share as not to bear. Give that we might live.
Show grace and not replace. Shine, so others He might find. Speaking in season and out of season. Speak to the atmosphere. This day shall we walk in his perfect peace, for greater is He (and these things that we have spoken) in us, than he that is in the world. AMEN.

APPLICATION

What things are going on around you that you may or may not desire in your presence at this time? Making a list and weeding out the non-essentials, helps me to focus on the things that are needed. Try it and see what happens.

OBSERVATION

"Let brotherly love continue. Be not forgetful to entertain strangers: for thereby some have entertained angels unawares." ***Hebrews 13: 1-2 (KJV)***

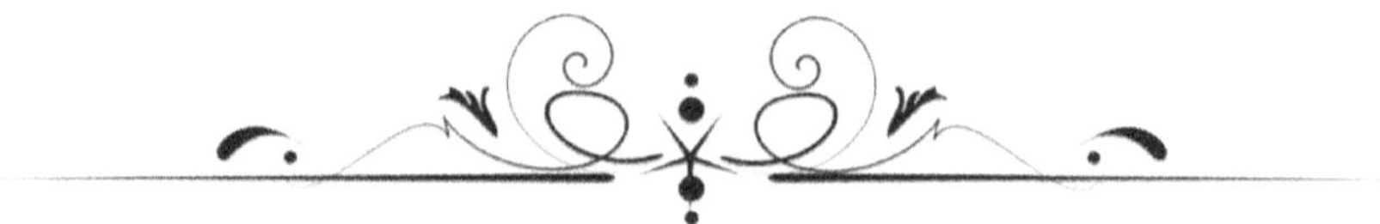

"LET LOVE ABIDE"

"*Every Person We Meet is a Prospective Soul for the Kingdom of God.*" This is our mantra at RHEMA Christian Fellowship Ministry Virtual Community Church. We strive each day to remember this and stay focused on others, rather than ourselves. For we know not whether we may cross paths with angels.

INTERPRETATION

Think about the people whose paths you will cross today.
Are they able to see you and hear what you say?

Someone may really be going through
Someone else may have a blessing just for you.
Someone may need a simple smile
Someone may have had to walk a hard, lonely mile.

Whatever your brother/sister may have had to endure
Offer them Christ through your living pure.
He is the way, the truth, and the life
Assure them that He is where they can release all of their strife.

Be careful of how you treat those you meet
For they too have a right to lie at His feet.

Every person we meet is a Kingdom prospect
It could be an angel you somehow neglect.

Jesus said, "*If I be lifted up, I will draw all men unto me*"
Aren't you glad he meant you as well as me!

Let love abide day in and day out
Treat all that you meet with a glorious shout.
Every person we meet is a Kingdom prospect
God's presentation through us has to come with the utmost of respect.

APPLICATION

Have you encountered anyone lately that made you think to yourself, "*This person needs Jesus?*" Did you take time to converse with them and find out if they REAL-ly knew him? List ways that you can approach the conversation of who Jesus is, and how important He is to salvation. Prepare to share with someone who might need to be educated on this.

OBSERVATION

"I will give you hidden treasures, riches stored in secret places, so that you may know that I am the Lord, the God of Israel, who summons you by name." ***Isaiah 45:3 (NIV)***

"TRUST ME, IT'S NOT TIME YET!"

In life when things are hidden from us, we sometimes tend to become disgruntled and we certainly don't trust those who are hiding them. God sometimes keeps the best things for us, from us, until such a time as He deems us ready for those very things. God knows us by name and character. Thus, He already knows what our response will be to the outcome. We have to wait for His appointed time to release certain things into our lives. When those treasures are released, we are better ablc to recognize them as blessings from the Lord.

INTERPRETATION

Many situations we face in life cause us pain and distrust. We find ourselves at odds with people we thought had our best interest at heart. Relationships may become distant due to them holding something back or not disclosing things to us. True friends and family recognize it may not be the opportune or right time to reveal what they have or know.

Do you realize sometimes we even question whether God has our best interest at heart? He needs us to recognize His role in our lives to include our part in trusting Him. I've often referred to this type of interaction as a REAL-ationship. For me, this comes down to recognizing that we have to give into our efforts to grow together in our interactions with God and each other. Our REAL-ationship becomes key in these situations. When we really know someone, we know what the other will or won't do or say. We know how they may or may not react under certain conditions. We have to spend time getting to know each other. This establishes and confirms that REAL-ationship.

Go ahead, try it. Spend time with the Father and get to know Him the way you want Him to know you. He has hidden treasures waiting that will be released at His will. He says that when they come forth, we will receive them, and know Him for who He is in our lives. He is Jehovah Jireh our provider. He reminds us to trust Him with our whole heart. When we do, we're able to accept if we must hear, "*It's not time yet*!"

APPLICATION

Take some time to examine the relationships that you have with others. Take an honest look at what you bring to each and think of ways you can do better in each one.

OBSERVATION

"And whatever you do, whether in word or deed, do it all in the name of the Lord Jesus, giving thanks to God the Father through him." **Colossians 3:17 (NIV)**

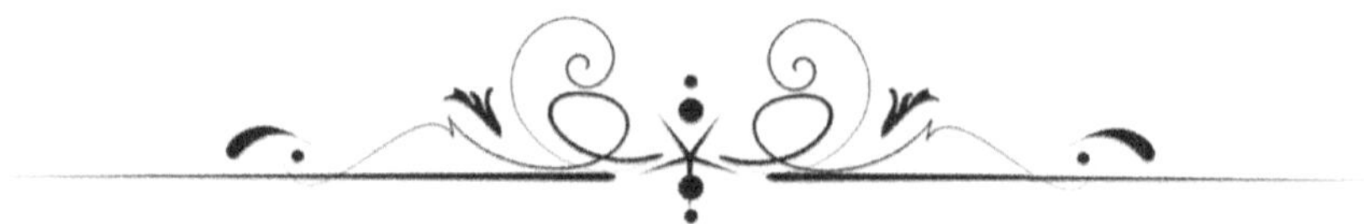

"THANKFUL TO THE FATHER"

There really is so much to be thankful for. Use your tongue, talents, and time today to show the Father and those around you, how thankful you are. Too often we go from day to day without ever saying these two simple words. "*Thank you.*" Two very simple words, yet they mean so much. Two simple words to show that you're grateful, that you're satisfied, that you've received something worth noting. But most of all these words mean that you're blessed. Why? Because, you're the recipient of something you need or want.

INTERPRETATION

"*Thank you*" is a humble response uttered after receiving something. Think about the times that you use these two words. Someone had to have shared something with you. Have you gotten any of these lately? Life, health, strength, assistance, increase, love, joy, peace, patience, kindness, a smile, a helping hand, a promotion, a healing, good fortune, a meal, lights on when you flip the switch, water flows when you turn on the faucet, a good nights' rest, and the list goes on.

God's will prevails when you receive one of these things. So, just say "*Thank you.*" Don't dwell on what people fail to do or what you don't have. Be thankful in the moments when people come through for you, and for how the Lord continues to bless you.

I always say, "*No matter what it looks like, sounds like, or feels like, God is in control. Thank God for the NOW.*" If you're reading this, know that you have a reason to say thank you, because you've evidently received the mercy of another day of life this morning.

APPLICATION

Take time today to think of what you can do to help someone look up to *Him*, and then look to you and say, "*Thank you*!"

OBSERVATION

"To everything there is a season, and a time to every purpose under the heaven." ***Ecclesiastes 3:1 (KJV)***

"THE FINAL PIECE"

Nothing in our lives happens by chance. God puts us in every situation for a reason and with a purpose. His Purpose. His Intention. Our lives are like a puzzle; the events of our lives are the pieces. Somehow, they must, and will fit together intentionally. Every piece has a purpose in its position. We may have to occasionally move pieces from one place to another: worship, friends, family, decisions, or obligations. It's up to us to figure out where each piece fits in best. Even those pieces that seem to fit elsewhere don't really work when out of place.

INTERPRETATION

Many years ago, my life took a turn. After several years of living in what society deems poverty, I landed a job working as a teacher's aide for the local school district. Mind you, I was raising my daughter as a single mother. I'd decided to return to school and get my degree to become a certified teacher. After a couple of semesters, I was presented with an opportunity to take part in the Pathways to Teaching Scholarship program offered at Armstrong Atlantic State University where I had enrolled. For my current situation at the time, this was the piece I needed.

The program itself, led by Dr. Evelyn B. Dandy (affectionately known to the scholars as Mama Dandy), developed into so many pieces of my unfinished puzzle; childcare, bill assistance, paid medical insurance, every Friday off to attend classes for "Scholars". Yes, I was now deemed a scholar. Going forward, there would be hard days and long nights; becoming scholar of the year; new traveling experiences; a grooming and perfecting of the 'pieces' for such a time as this. When the pieces of the puzzle of life don't or won't fit, we start pushing and forcing to make them fit. Looking at things from a different angle may help get things into perspective. The pieces begin to come together and fall so easily into the right places. Today, I am a retired Assistant Principal with more than 30 years of educational experience with the same school district.

My time, my season, my puzzle pieces are still evolving. In the end the final piece in place will bring it all together. But God! After many years of looking for the end to my beginning in all the wrong places, I realize He was there all the time. Jesus Christ, the final piece to our lifelong puzzle. I will continue to strive as I long to see the day when my final piece is put in place. For now, I'm going to keep living, keep it going, and keep the pieces moving.

APPLICATION

Think of a time in your life when you felt that something was just a coincidence. Can you see now how God's hand was in it?

POETIC PIECES FROM THE PAST

"A Tribute To Our Mother"

As we look back and realize where God has brought us from, we stop and thank Him graciously for all that He has done.

He placed each of us in your life and gave us one another, and even when we caused you strife, you stayed right there Dear Mother.

You could have said, "I quit, I'm done!"
You could have said, "I'm through."
You could have walked away and left,
feeling there was nothing else to do.

But Mother, oh Mother, you stayed and prayed
with God right by your side.
Giving your will and way to Him,
allowing our Father to be your guide.

Now for these things we thank you, and give our
Lord the praise.
But most of all we love you and will for the rest of our
days.

A tribute in the program booklet of E. Larry Mcduffie and the Savannah Community Choir's anniversary booklet in (1988); mother served as a member more than 50 years.

"An Encouragement"

Mom, God gave you a dozen roses, each special in its own way. He asked you to nurture and keep them and watch them from day to day.

As He gave them to you, He told you, to do the best that you could. For one day He'd have to take them back, when they'd proven all that they should.

The first that He gave was artistic and bright,
he was strong in his will; he was strong in his might. You called his name Charles and showed him the way, that he needed to live each and every day.

As Charles grew older you allowed him to know
he could make his own choices in which way he should go. He didn't always choose the road you knew was best. But deep down inside, he knew he'd have to pass God's test.

So, he ventured and wandered, and experienced the world. Always considerate of others as he traveled along, even forgiving of those who treated him wrong.

Charles grew older and wiser and finally learned
that a true place in God was the thing that he yearned. So, he gave his life over to Jesus our King, and the angels began to rejoice and to sing.

God looked down and saw that his first rose had bloomed, so, the angels prepared a special place in the upper room. And, on Wednesday, November the third of this year, He reached down and held Charles in His bosom so dear.

Just remember as you continue nurturing the other eleven, Charles awaits for all of us by God's side in Heaven.

An encouragement to my mom in the loss and memory of her first born, Charles David Houston; the eldest of the even dozen that God had blessed her with (1993). Today the other eleven still stand strong. Mother has gone on.

"Live Out The Dream"

Doctor
Learn, love, care.
Allow the healing to begin.
Clear it up, make it better.
Dream the dream and you will win.
Dr. King didn't stop because the way wasn't clear.
He remained strong and brave, healing all of the fears.

Lawyer
Define, defend, and explain it your way,
the dream is still alive in each of you today.
Justice, peace, equality you'll get
only if the dream you never forget.
Know for sure what he meant,
and what his dream represents.
Keep yourselves on the right track
there is no time, no time to go back.

Cosmetologist
Dress it up, keep it tight,
straight and steady is what's right.
Looking up, never down,
dream of many smiles, not frowns.
Looking good is okay,
but we know not, the day.
So fix it up, keep it straight,
the dreamer's dream cannot wait.

Sports Player
Moving fast, slowing down, are you running for your crown? Homerun! Touch down! Get the dream up off the ground. Hole in one, server up, who'll take home the winning cup? Play your ball, dream it all,
do it right and you won't fall.

Teachers
Reading, writing, arithmetic,
hold on to the dream that you have picked.
Teachers come and teachers go, but this one thing we know for sure. The dreamer dreams and dreams come true, so teach them to become a dreamer too.
Show love and care where they're concerned,
and each of your students can and will learn.

Ministers
Jesus Christ gave His life, took our sins away.
Dr. King's was sacrificed, so the dream is here to stay.
Someone's listening you will see.
The dream is as plain as can be.
So spread the news everywhere, over here and over there.
Preach and pray, and sing for evermore, every dream can open doors.

Every One
Keep it live, keep it fair,
dream the dream, if you dare.
Martin did it, Martin tried,
and for that very thing he died.
But the dream yet remains,
in our hearts, it was not in vain.
Live out the dream, if you dare.
keep it live everywhere!

Live Out, Live Out the Dream

Written in encouragement to the youth of the Peaceful Zion Missionary Baptist Church to be anything they desired to be in life. Shared during the dual celebration of Black History Month and Martin Luther King's Remembrance (2002).

NOTES AND REFLECTIONS

ABOUT THE AUTHOR

Pastor Carzadean B. Harris, known to her family and close friends as "Josie", is a native of Savannah, GA, where she currently resides with her husband Mr. William M. Harris. She is the mother of one daughter, Jolene J. Baker and son, Franklin W. "Trey" Butler, III. She is the 9th child and 8th daughter of Mrs. Lucille E. Tanksley, and the daughter of the late Mr. Joseph A. Baker, Jr.

Pastor Carzadean as she has become affectionately known to her members and followers answered the call to ministry in 2001. She was further trained in ministry under the leadership of the late Rev. Robert H. Thorpe at the Peaceful Zion Missionary Baptist Church (PZBC) in Savannah, GA and ordained in 2004. She presently serves as the Pastor and Co-Founder of the present-day RHEMA Christian Fellowship Ministry Virtual Community Church, since 2009, alongside her husband. She served as a faithful member of the Grammy nominated, The Savannah Community Choir under the direction of Mr. E. Larry McDuffie for more than 30 years. She is the co-owner and operator of Carz-In-Christ Creations, Inc., a local printing company in the Savannah area.

Carzadean is a 1980 graduate of the Alfred Ely Beach High School in Savannah, GA. In 1984 she obtained a degree in Practical Nursing from Savannah-Vocational Technical School where she graduated with honors. She earned a Bachelor of Science degree in Education from Armstrong Atlantic State College in 1997, a Master of Education-Early Childhood Education from Armstrong Atlantic State University in 2002, and a degree in Advanced Graduate Studies in Educational Leadership from Cambridge College in 2009. During her tenure with Savannah-Chatham County Public School District, for more than 30 years, she has received numerous accomplishments and awards and held many positions; Paraprofessional, Certified Classroom Teacher (3rd-5th grades), Technology Lab Instructor, Math Lab Instructor, America's Choice Math Coach, Academic Coach, and finally Assistant Principal for more than 9 years. She retired August 1, 2020.

She received nominations for Sallie Mae 1st Year Teacher of the Year (1997) and Teacher of the Year (2002) at Spencer Elementary School. She presented at the 11th Annual Week of the Young Child, Armstrong Atlantic State University (2002), 6th Annual Regional Middle School Collaborative Conference (2003) Coastal Georgia Center, was nominated for the National Council of Teachers of Mathematics (NCTM) Award (2002) and was also featured in a Learning in Motion's video, Interviews of Math Coaches, America's Choice Math Program (2002).

Carzadean was selected by a screening committee to the Dewitt Wallace Reader's Digest Pathways to Teaching Program at Armstrong State College (1993) directed by

Dr. Evelyn B. Dandy; awarded the Pathways to Teaching Scholar of The Year (1997); published as a research assistant (for Dr. Evelyn B. Dandy) in the RNT (Recruiting New Teachers) Publication, Preparing Highly Qualified Paraeducators (2005); presenter on several occasions at educational conferences in Atlanta, GA, Virginia Beach, VA., Charleston, SC., and Jacksonville, FL.

Her favorite scripture says, "Jabez cried out to the God of Israel, "*Oh, that you would bless me Oh Lord indeed, and enlarge my territory! Let your hand be with me and keep me from evil.*" And God granted that which He requested. **1 Chronicles 4:10**.

Her scripture of refuge and daily encouragement says, "*For I know the plans I have for you," declares the Lord, "plans to prosper you and not to harm you, plans to give you hope and a future.*"
Jeremiah 29:11

WE WANT TO HEAR FROM YOU

If this book has made a difference in your life I would be delighted to hear about it!

Leave a review on Amazon.com

BOOK AUTHOR CARZADEAN TO SPEAK AT YOUR NEXT EVENT

Send an email to: **carzinchrist333@gmail.com**

FOLLOW AUTHOR CARZADEAN ON SOCIAL MEDIA

Facebook:
www.facebook.com/Carzadean Baker Harris (Author Carzadean)

Linked In:
www.linkedin.com/in/author-carzadean-b-harris-ed-s-358a55108

Instagram:
www.instagram.com/carzinchrist333

www.whenheavenspeakspublishing.com

Made in United States
North Haven, CT
08 December 2023

45354998R00059